Hidden Truths Within

Truths, Teachings & Meditations

BRAHM

Hidden Truths Within – 1st ed.
Truths, teachings & meditations
Brahm

Cover Design by AlyBlue Media, LLC
Interior Design by AlyBlue Media LLC
Published by AlyBlue Media, LLC
Copyright © 2021 by AlyBlue Media All rights reserved. No part of this publication may be reproduced, distributed or transmitted in any form or by any means, without prior written permission of the publisher.

ISBN: 978-1-944328-98-6
AlyBlue Media, LLC
Ferndale, WA 98248
www.AlyBlueMedia.com

This book is designed to provide informative narrations to readers. It is sold with the understanding that the author or publisher is not engaged to render any type of psychological, legal, or any other kind of professional advice. The content is the sole expression and opinion of the author. No warranties or guarantees are expressed or implied by the choice to include any of the content in this book. Neither the publisher nor the author shall be liable for any physical, psychological, emotional, financial, or commercial damages including but not limited to special, incidental, consequential or other damages.

PRINTED IN THE UNITED STATES OF AMERICA

Dedication

For my guru, and for those who receive
benefit from these teachings.

Contents

Introduction vii

PART 1

1	The First Teaching	3
2	The Second Teaching	5
3	The Third Teaching	9
4	The Fourth Teaching	15
5	The Fifth Teaching	17
6	The Sixth Teaching	21
7	The Seventh Teaching	23
8	The Eighth Teaching	25
9	The Ninth Teaching	31
10	The Tenth Teaching	35
11	The Eleventh Teaching	37
12	The Twelfth Teaching	39
13	The Thirteenth Teaching	43
14	The Fourteenth Teaching	47

PART 2

15	The Fifteenth Teaching	53
16	The Sixteenth Teaching	59
17	The Seventeenth Teaching	63
18	The Eighteenth Teaching	67

19	The Nineteenth Teaching	69
20	The Twentieth Teaching	73
21	The Twenty-first Teaching	77
22	The Twenty-second Teaching ..	79
23	The Twenty-third Teaching	81

PART 3

24	The Twenty-fourth Teaching ...	85
25	The Twenty-fifth Teaching	89
26	The Twenty-sixth Teaching	93
27	The Twenty-seventh Teaching .	97
28	The Twenty-eight Teaching	101
29	The Twenty-ninth Teaching	103

Introduction

The following writings resulted from a profound experience I had one summer evening quite some time ago. The experience came about when I had just got into bed and was experiencing a high and strong vibration of spiritual energy within my body. After some time of lying and feeling this energy, I felt a strong urge to focus all my attention on an area toward the top and back of my head.

Suddenly I found myself sitting in a beautiful wooded area within a clearing of a forest. It was night time and a wood fire was burning quietly in front of me. I was sitting on the ground cross-legged looking at the fire and surrounding forest. I then looked to my left and there was a beautifully still, serene older man of light-brown skin. He was dressed in white robes, sitting cross-legged, with his eyes closed, also facing the fire. I had never seen this man before and he was radiating a deep peace and appeared to be in a deep meditative state. We sat in silence for some time and I felt a strong sense of a deep communication happening between us. This communication was not through words or thoughts, rather it felt like a deep love and knowing between our innermost selves. I sat experiencing this for a few minutes and then naturally came back to the awareness of my bed and bedroom.

Over the next couple days, I began feeling a strong presence within and around me, and some messages started entering my mind in a way I had never experienced. I intuitively knew these were messages from that same man. The strongest and most memorable of these were the words, "I will always be with you".

It was during this time when I first felt a strong urge to write one word at a time through feeling, without any thought or knowledge of what word would follow the previous word I was typing. I would feel a pull to come back to this type of writing over the coming months and years.

Several years later, I was meditating when I had another deep inner experience. This time I found myself at a beautiful rock pool, which was not of this earthly realm. It was a place of extreme bliss and beauty, free of physical form. Everything appeared almost translucent and luminescent with a radiant glow. The area included a deep, tranquil, blue rock pool surrounded by open rock walls. A peaceful natural light not of this world illuminated the area. Small light-green trees and colourful flowers inhabited the surroundings. The air was still, and the peace within was intoxicatingly blissful. It was here we met for a second time.

During this experience, we swam in the rock pool quietly, though extremely present in each other's company. There again was a strong sense of silent communication and connection free of words. I stayed within this experience for some time before naturally becoming aware of my physical surroundings once again.

The following writings are the truths, teachings and poetic meditations that have come through this type of writing over the years. You may want to open any page at random and focus on a few of the teachings, or read from front to back or anything in between. They have given me a huge amount of guidance and inspiration, I hope they do for you, too.

BRAHM

PART 1

CHAPTER ONE

The First Teaching

How do I overcome?

Breathe.

Let be what will be.

Hold close to that which is true.

Remember, it is all perfect; what you are doing right now is perfect. What others are doing right now is perfect for them and perfect for you.

Challenges will be faced but can be overcome.

Leave the knowing to the Self and let the mind rest easy in the knowledge that it is all within perfection.

Trust in what is true, what is pure, what is love.

Notice the mind, notice what is not true, notice you can stay within your One true Self and not let the mind overtake.

Trust and patience are virtues that will serve you well. Do not let negative emotion rule, for what is gained. You have grown through pain, now grow through love.

All is perfect right now.

All is necessary.

It is not something your mind can understand, so stay in true presence, free from thought.

Love all, including those your mind has negative thoughts or emotions for. Live and breathe through it. It is not always easy but you are growing, you are learning, you can master what it is that is interfering, that which is clinging, that which is no longer necessary.

Hold onto what is true, to the deepest feelings inside you. Be cautious of the mind and what it is creating. Love.

CHAPTER TWO

The Second Teaching

There is only one way to be set free.

Breathe . . . Hold still . . . Look . . . Listen . . .

Leave your own mind, and forget.

Sit still in peace, holding true to within.

Be One with the Source, the truth, the knowing.

Trust in the Divine.

Leave your mind to being the mind.

The path can be dark, the path can be lit, just trust in following the path.

But how do you do this?

Breathe. Hold still. Trust. Drop into presence.

The knowing is within.

The feeling is within.

The mind is not stopping access to Source; it is all how it should be.

Say yes to all. Say yes to the suffering, say yes to the ego, say yes to the journey.

The flowers dripped the truth of what lies in waiting, in searching, in seeking that, which is. The truth of the flowers was not.

Suffering is, and will be, for how long it is necessary.

Pain is there to wake you up, to show you the way of negation of the mind, to realise the destructive power of the mind and the emotions. It is there to help you be free of the conflictions of it, and that which it creates.

Love all, feel the Oneness with all, know that the mind is seeking separateness, seeking pain, seeking conflict, seeking solution. Solution the mind is not built for.

You are feeling what you need to feel, thinking what you need to think, learning what you need to learn. Life's outer purpose for you will call when it calls. Until then, follow your depth within as best as you are able and meant to.

CHAPTER THREE

The Third Teaching

You will realise what can be
realised when it is realised.

You must leave what is to be, when what is to be is through the One.

There is more than thought that reigns supreme.

There is only One, and One is not the only One but the One.

Will is not to be without a need for reckoning. For reckoning is to reason that which love is to hate.

You must lie within before you can lie without, through the One that is.

What will be, need not be and cannot be, should it not be what will be and was meant to be.

There are many more lives of glory left to be discovered.

Hold true to what your knowing purpose is, has become, will be, or will not be.

What is done is not done when it can be done through the eyes of the Supreme.

Leave only what is necessary when questioning what is to be done, when it is done.

There are many more paths of discovery that can be achieved through holding onto the One.

Show what is shown when it is shown.

Never say never and never understand never, for never will never be never.

There is hope in what is to become the One of all creation in depths yet unfathomable to us all.

When holding what is true, never hold onto that which is holding you from the true path of the One Divine.

With arms outstretched, leave room for what is to be, what will be, and what has always been.

Surpass the need, the desire, the want, the craving, the desperation for a calling from within. For what is within cannot be without, and will always be the One true love of the One destiny held within the One that is and will be forevermore. Amen.

Will is.

Hold true to what is all within the One, and the One will show its wonders at the times when all is good, when all is full, when all is within what is without.

Leave the nevers of the past free to shelter in the nevers that will be. For the nevers need not surface on the wills and the ideas around the creation of what is. What will be, will surface through the One true creation held within the One, within the all and the all within the One.

There is freedom through the self-expression of the One, the love, the only, the holy spirit of creation and wonder.

When lighting foreign paths, hold what is and will be through firm and able hands made smooth through love and Oneness.

There can be only One when all there can be is through One.

When leaves of fall leave uncertainty within, hold deep to what is, to what will be, to the unbridled cosmos of the Oneness plane of the unconscious desire to be within the One: that is without the separateness of desire; for this will no longer be of truth, and never has nor never will reign supreme of the Oneness heart of the Lord, the all, the us, the them, the totality of truth, the past, the future and the current totality of existence. Amen.

When holding nigh to what is, what is, is to be not examined but what is, is to be desired through systems of the Oneness of what is and is in itself that which is in all.

Holding this high above the lights of the blissful, there will be only a need for the lights to be lit through the passion, through the love, through the Oneness of all and the all that is the One.

Should a man fall from the grace, should a man be struck with shame, should a man be held from love, should a man be hurt with all pain, should a man be sent from the life of the One, then what is and what is not shall not be clear, nor shall it seemingly be without that which is the One, the Only, the Divine.

There is no need for the desires, for the ills, for the serenity and dullness that is separateness. For the Divine holds high through pillars of the Source, through the grace, the beauty, the truth of what is, what shall be and what has always been, but will never be shown until the time of the great unravelling of the Divine with all its presence and joy and beauty and love and wonder the world has been blessed and will be forever blessed to witness, to be with, to hold, to live in and to be.

Leave not what is left but hold dear to what there is within the soulness of the One, within the soulness of the All, within the soulness of the Divine, forever present.

Peace forevermore will be there when it is there, where it will be. For it will be when life is One and One is life, and all that is bliss, is pure, is joy, is love, is beauty, is splendour, is far and wide and deep and high and all held dear with free-loving arms through the Divine, the One, the Beautiful, the Creator of the loveness, the Oneness and fullness of the harmonious life that will always be with the One, the One of all, the all within One.

You are me as I am you, and me through you is you through me. So me with you is you with me, and will be and will forever be as One.

Purpose is found when thoughts are silenced through prayer, through meditation, through love and true wisdom and the faith that can be and will be the One.

A path is formed when light is shone from the depths and the heights of what is. And what is, is held through the One, the One that is the creation of us all, and all is within the likeness of not only creation but the Source as well. Amen.

CHAPTER FOUR

The Fourth Teaching

> What is it you're looking for,
> waiting for?

How can one be open through not holding onto the Oneness of life?

Deadness is only felt when living is found separate from being.

When dreaming is seemingly lost in thoughts, life is lost in doing.

Disharmony can only be felt through resisting the whole.

Every present moment carries inherently the choice of being or not being.

When one leaves thought, one brings a new life force into play.

Hold close and true to Source, and know with all your heart it will lead you perfectly.

Look at the emotions, look at the thoughts for what they are: remnants of a past consciousness.

Leave open possibility.

Hold deep to within: to presence.

Trust in that, let it guide you, let me guide you.

Trust that and you will be free, you will become One with Source.

There is no rush, there are no questions of future, only of your purpose right now.

Your purpose right now is always and will always be to trust the deep Oneness, the love Oneness, the totality within you, within all.

Your purpose right now is to be in Oneness-heart, staying in the place of trust deep within.

Love you, love all, love is.

CHAPTER FIVE

The Fifth Teaching

Hello, my friend. Welcome back.

You must now look forward and high.

The heavens will await.

You need not suffer any longer.

You need not look for pain.

You may be free.

You may be full of love.

Look toward those who hold great strength within.

Those who can inspire, those who attract.

Those who love life.

Your journey never stopped, nor never will.

You trust in God, and God will trust in you.

It is One in the same.

Look up and feel the lifeforce flowing back, flowing through, flowing with all of the eternal Oneness-life.

You need not worry about a thing, just trust in the Oneness.

Feel the trust resonating within you.

Feel the presence of the eternal, the eternal present.

Be interested, be curious, laugh at the workings of your mind and its need for ridicule.

It is creation through energy, which has no use other than showing the need for the use of life energy, use of the Oneness energy.

Keep learning, keep desiring, keep fulfilling your purpose.

Hold close to your trust in God and His wonders and His workings through you.

Access to life energy is number one; everything external then falls where it should, through the life energy.

There are no problems, no failures, only what is.

You can only trust in God and trust you are carrying out and experiencing everything that is required, regardless of what the thoughts and emotions are trying to do.

They do not know, they love to try and seemingly interfere with God's direction although this is impossible as all, including the most destructive thoughts, are at One with God.

This does not mean you do not have choice, for choice is all you have. Know that every choice is the right one as you have surrendered to living through God, and God through you.

CHAPTER SIX

The Sixth Teaching

Hello my friend. What is it that I'm feeling?

Only you can answer that

It feels like fear, it feels like a block in my mind. Why would I be feeling this?

You are feeling this because you are scared to accept, you are scared to let go. You no longer need what it is you think you need, yet you are not prepared to let go. Get prepared. Let go.

How can I do this?

Through going deeply into what it is you are feeling. Go into it totally openly, totally without resistance and in full surrender.

How do I do this?

Sitting or lying down, take your attention and put it first on the feeling of blockage in your mind. Spread light to it, explore it fully with this light, feel the attention going through it, in full non-resistance and acceptance. Do this until you intuitively know to stop. Then follow the energy down into the body and put the bright light of attention on the feelings within the body.

Surrender fully to the feeling.

Tell it you have surrendered.

Tell it you are ready now for your mind to be clear, your heart to be open, and to feel at peace.

Keep bringing the powerful bright light of attention back to bathe in whenever it drifts back to mind thoughts. Concentrate it powerfully first in the feeling in the head, then follow it down to the feeling within and bathe in it, and turn it up.

Say: I no longer resist, I fully surrender, I am ready to let go. I am ready for peace and presence.

CHAPTER SEVEN

The Seventh Teaching

One love.

Fullness of life through fullness of being.

When holding dear to the Oneness, plain miracles not only become possible, they intermittently occur. Through realising what can unfold through being at one with what is can not only give full purpose and meaning to life, but also give true joy to living.

To access what is, let go of what is not: the falsehoods seen as real. Let go of mind creation; see it clearly through the light of being for what it really is. Absolute fiction. Absolutely unnecessary. Absolute needlessness.

You need to watch without a judgmental or analytical eye. You need to watch then let go, watch then let go. Fully surrender in the knowing it cannot harm you and holds no truth. Do this always.

Always remember and trust that everything is of absolute perfection. Every action, every thought, every evil, every good, is all God. For God is all and all is God. All is perfection. Trust there are no mistakes and trust completely in following the Oneness-heart. Any doubt is doubt from the mind, doubt through God, doubt to awaken.

Trust. Trust. Trust.

Love. Love. Love.

Start showing this trust in the Oneness. Set free the demons of mind and body created by the falsehood of ego. Move into the realm of reality. Trust in the now. Watch. Listen. Look. Feel. Hold onto within with full love and attention.

You are getting close, my friend. You are almost ready, you are almost whole to receiving what is.

Love always.

Amen.

CHAPTER EIGHT

The Eighth Teaching

Hi, my friend.

How do I let go of my ego?

Forget letting go of anything. Forget the word ego. Forget your mental conceptions of what you perceive to be your ego and mind.

What is it you actually want?

I want to feel my true self, and act through it.

I want to have a happy and peaceful mind.

I want to be free from pain.

Do not concentrate on what to drop or be free of. Concentrate on the positives. Forget about concentrating on the negatives.

Be free of wanting, of needing. Allow full surrender and acceptance to what is, and fuel the desire to be true Self.

You are not your mind

You will feel very different very soon. Hold close to faith and truth and love and the knowing.

Be One, be free.

When you realise the truth of what is, hold it close to the living, close to the Oneness-heart.

When feeling the pain and confusion of intense dwelling in mind, use the feelings, use the thoughts to assist in realising that it is not you, that it will never be you. You can set Self-free through holding dear to the truth within. Trust in this.

Trust and be, be and live, live and trust.

There is no need to hold onto the trappings of the mind any longer.

Ask self, ask me, ask the Oneness of all.

Purpose will be clear when it is clear, when it is awakened.

Awaken the purpose within through awakening within. Do this through letting go of the past, through letting go of the future, through dwelling intensely in the now and, most importantly, putting full faith and trust on the true Self within the true Oneness: the truth of all truths.

Confidence and full trust in following true Self is gained through beginning to follow consciously. You are always following the path of what is unconsciously, but bring the light of consciousness to it, and infinite depth, wonder, trust and joy will work through your being.

When following true Self, put full awareness on the mind and the fear of emotions. See them for what they are: a fantasy created through ego, a fantasy created where no creation is required.

Step out of comfort through following the truth, and live and become what is truth, what is love, what it is to be present within Oneness, the Oneness of all.

You will know you will be able to make life decisions when trust, full trust, is felt and held dear.

Let go of mind. Hold onto the infinite depths of being. Through interaction with the Oneness of others, the Oneness of self deepens.

When being with what is, there will initially be a strong pull from mind to leave what is, to comment, to judge, to raise doubt, to question, to create counterproductive negative thoughts and emotions. Just notice this, smile and drop back into above mind.

Your outer play with life can bring joy and love to within when within is held close to the truth and Oneness.

The key thing is to know that there are no mistakes, there are no problems on the level of being. Play with scenarios, get out and start trying things, through following within.

If there is doubt whether to do something, whether you do it or don't do it does not matter; it is all perfect.

If you feel a pull to do it, do it. If you don't, then don't, but whatever decision is made is the right one, as there is no right and wrong.

If mind perceived negative experience comes about, there will be opportunity to grow and learn from it. If positive experience is found, learning and growth will also happen. It is all as it is, your personal outward actions have no importance with true Self. So become involved in what is, and be free of mind and ego.

CHAPTER NINE

The Ninth Teaching

Peace is the innermost realm of being.
Peace can be with all, all with peace.

When held onto without neediness or grasping of any kind, peace is pure. It is the utmost, it is the God within.

When it is enjoyed and held within next to the Oneness-heart of all, great beauty will reign.

Leaving forth all of mind's troubles, all of mind's emotions, all of mind's destructiveness, is done when the knower becomes the known.

Setting forth onto the miracles of being, with life, with the Oneness of all that is, the journey is full of joy, of wonder, of great passion and love.

Outer experiences are all perfect, all necessary. Growth is found in many forms under many circumstances within many experiences; all beautiful in their necessity within the One.

What is cannot be, without God's grace.

Love what is within the inner and outer, and hold forever closer in the trust embrace of the Divine.

Become forever more aware of the workings of the mind. When mind sneaks through back passages, shine great light of awareness on it as soon as can be. For light transmutes the darkness of mind into the lightness of being. Into the beauty of that which is the One.

Forget any judgment of mind activity as good or bad, positive or negative. It is there for pure reasons far beyond the reaches of the intellectual understanding. All thoughts, all emotions hold beauty as awakeners, as realisations, as signposts to the utmost of perfection within.

Fully give over to what is; feel no fear to current mind experiences. Shine the courage of welcome and embrace to each and every one. Surrender and full acceptance leaves no glue for lower negative vibrational mind forms to take hold, and leaves full room for the love, joy and positivity to run deep.

You are doing well, my friend. Here are some further pointers and aspirations:

- Show love, compassion, and understanding through its emanation free of mind.

- The mind is growing desperate, the more desperate the closer to true freedom. Hold firm to the Oneness-heart as the mind takes its last stand.

- The mind and ego grow heavy with the dread of losing the power over form. This heaviness, this density, this despair can be worked through the body, through the being, and the transmutation can and will unravel.

- True self is coming forth, do not let the death rattles of the mind gain power over what is. If this is done however, it is of, course, all perfection.

- You need not be ill at ease with what is happening, for it is beautiful. It is perfect and it is all in line with realising the Oneness of all, all One for God, all of God.

CHAPTER TEN

The Tenth Teaching

Hold deep to what is. That is all.

When at ease with what is, you cannot be without the one true source of love, of creativity, of the knowing of all creation.

You need not think, when thinking is what is causing blocks, thinking is what is destructive: it is all your mind. Outside of this is all peace, all love, all Oneness.

Leave what is to be left, and give it up to the Oneness of all.

You can do no wrong in the eyes of the Lord.

Follow trueness, follow Oneness, and follow the depths within.

Have the courage to lie in what it is that is causing pain. Do not dwell, do not judge, go deeply into it and shine the bright light of awareness on it. Accept it, choose with all your being to move through it. Choose happiness, joy and delight.

CHAPTER ELEVEN

Eleventh Teaching

*Hi, I'm not sure, what do I do,
how do I find peace and Oneness?*

You need to hold onto the Oneness of what is.

You are not allowing life to lead you. You are not allowing the flow of creation.

When living whole, there is no need for resistance, there is no need for pain and suffering, there is only what is true.

You must trust.

But how do I do this?

Allow all pain, know it as delusion, let go of resisting that which has already been.

Become open to all that is, and all that is, is One.

When learning the ways of the mind, treat it lightly. There is nothing needed to learn other than full surrender and acceptance.

It is now time to let go. Suffering has been, and now it is time for the joy of awakening, it is time to be, to be with One, to be with True Self.

Personality, thoughts and feelings will still be there, but at a lighter more free level of your consciousness.

It is time, it is time, it is time. It is time to awaken consciously, there is no need to delay with suffering, unease and despair in the hope of feeling better eventually. Now is the time, and the time is now.

Start following the Oneness within, and all will unravel with beauty.

CHAPTER TWELVE

Twelfth Teaching

Needing time cannot free what it is
you are escaping from within and
without.

There can only be the need for awakening when all is surrendered and all is loved, all is fully accepted.

Ills may lie within the opportunity that presents itself to discover the full truth of what is.

Holding through resistance to those things which are causing phantom fear are not only destructive powers of will but also the life sapping energy of dread; of full life mind control.

To move into full presence, full aliveness, one can only leave the mind through surrender, acceptance and love, and through leaving the mind the will of life flows through what is, and joy and love and happiness is welcomed with loving arms into the realm of the Oneness plane.

To live in the body is to live in the grace of God within. To live in the entrapment of mind is to live without. Without the joys and peace and trueness of what is.

When trust is given, trust is received. Trust with God, and what is, is once again held together through being.

The noticing of energy in mind and body is beautiful. The energy flowing into parts of the mind when panic, fear, resistance is felt—give this full awareness, be one with it consciously. Do not try to escape it, as it is there, and cannot cease to be through unconsciousness.

To find true peace, find true trust within the energy of the body and the flow of life. Leave minds ills behind through full awareness and conscious surrender and acceptance.

To carry one's energy in the mind, be it negative, is like carrying around an energy-sucking vampire within, when at any time you can choose to release the vampire's teeth through consciously going into the body and giving full conscious awareness to the thoughts, feelings and emotions currently being experienced and then entering the life energy within, where truth and love and true life itself, through God, exists and lives.

There is a need for the mind to pull, to trick into large importance—become fully aware of the trickery and notice becoming absorbed in it. Practice consciously trying to become fully taken over by it— this is the key to full mastery of mind. Where is the energy? When there is awareness of the mind wanting to take over: notice it, surrender to it and actively try to push more energy, create more thoughts and feelings of negative value consciously. Then watch what happens. This is the art of gaining.

To live in harmony with what is, one must acknowledge that all is flowing effortlessly, and mind resistance is futile. Know the next move, go within, then act—whether mind perceives it and it results as a wrong decision, this is irrelevant. All flows, all can be learning and experiencing life.

To live like I, one must follow the heart and tap into the life energy source to provide the will, the strength, the courage and the knowing of what is to be the awakening.

The mind cannot imagine what is held in store for you, my friend.

Now allow life's energy to rest deep within and begin to gain back the life energy that has been poisoned in the ill trappings of the egoic mind. Do this through conscious awareness and with the full, total and trusting knowledge that right now this moment, this truth, is just as it should be.

CHAPTER THIRTEEN

Thirteenth Teaching

Hello, my friend. Are you still at the rock pool?

Does it matter? Welcome into the space dimension of no time, where no time is to be the awareness of the utmost and the integration through presence of all that is.

When all is found, all is lost and holding true to your past of no time within, there can be no longer a self of ignorance.

When all is within the Oneness plane, all is within and without. All is total, all is complete.

When you are no longer with the ignorant heart, all can be felt within and without. All of existence is now One existence of the true Oneness, totality of existence.

Leave all suffering, leave all doubts of the mind and its ignorance. There is no place, no need for the forest of thoughts, where one tree at a time can be cut or planted.

All there is, is all there will be, was and can be. There is no other moment than this moment, and when this can be felt what else can be of meaning to your life, as it is as it is, was and will be.

Leaving this to be with that is what is now needed. Do not purify the self through thought of the need, the want or the requirement. All that is needed is awareness of the Soul, of the Oneness, of the Truth behind all of creation.

You are not, and what is not, cannot be undone.

Through the longing that is ego, the mind of destruction can freely take grip of what the mind wishes. Let go of this grip. Let go of the need for desire, for the need of control. Do this through mind awareness. Through letting fullness take what is and showing the path.

This path need not be as a path is known, but this path is within, without, inside and outside all that is and all at one moment: this moment.

Can you be holding true to what is within and without? Can you say what needs to be said within and without of all things, and where that can only be of no things?

Leaving behind and leaving the front of all suffering hearts of the mind, learn through loving what can only be in this moment of creation.

You do not need this life of pleasures, this life of cultured mind-based additions to this nothingness field of life. Live, love the life of the One through One, and One can only be seen and felt as One. One is not the life of leisure, the life of desire and false fulfilment. When all is known to be natural, there is only one step along the path of infinite love and kindness.

As long as thoughts of this and that, of that and this roam freely, there can be no Oneness-heart felt on Oneness-planes of love and truth and all that is.

You are that Oneness that all of this is. Take it within and without, love it dearly. That is all there is.

Stay strong within. Stay weak without. No longer does the mind need to take on a charge it can no longer service or control.

Few of us have what needs to be accomplished and accommodated. You need not want to be this or to be that, just be.

CHAPTER FOURTEEN

Fourteenth Teaching

Hello, my friend.

When all is well, there is no need for that which can leave behind that which is unobserved.

When all is well, there remains no desire, no wanting, no craving, no expectations of what has been, what is and what will be.

Leave your heart to join the heart. The heart that is One, the heart that is of all. Trust within this Oneness-heart, and all is well.

What is required is what is shown, and what is shown is when this moment presents itself.

Can you walk among those within ignorant minds, within confused hearts?

Can you embrace all? Can you be at one with all that is?

This is the secret to living a full life. Living the Oneness life of all creation. Hold true to that which is this Oneness life. Trust. Pause. Go deep. Stay silent. Love, live and learn through Oneness.

To stay within truth takes no time at all. To stay within ignorance takes all the time in the universe. To stay within love takes depth, takes power, and takes no thing within all things.

Through looking deep all that you are is all that is, and through this isness One can be felt, through the Oneness of all that is.

You are to the universe that which water is to the stream. The water flows this way and that but remains within the totality of the stream of life.

When all that can be felt can be felt within, then nothing remains to be accomplished. Can you accept the truth of all that can be accepted?

To see or not to see is not the question remaining to be answered. The question remaining to be answered is why there is no cause for concern. The answer is all that is, and all that is, is to be in Oneness within the perfection that can only be through the here and now.

The sacred truths of existence need not be answered through thought. The sacred truths are as follows:

All peace will come when all peace is sought.

All truth is there when no longer a mind can interfere.

You have what is and what is, is all requirements held within.

When walking along the path of light take no heed for the darkness. For the darkness of ignorance can take hold of no light. For the darkness of fear can grasp onto nothing lit within the flames of the heart.

The sacredness of being within Oneness is for all of creation, and all of creation is all there is, and all there is cannot be tarnished with any brush of what can only be perceived as that which no longer serves us.

Feel the light within all. Feel the touch of the warmth of creation. Feel the Oneness of all that is through the knowing of true love. This knowing can be known by trusting deep in the perfection of all that is.

To stay within the wonders of the universe one can deeply be.

There is no other time for the depth of Self to be discovered. There is no other time for the love of all things to be manifested.

You and only you, One and only One.

Trust where no trust can be seen, live like no lives have been lived.

PART 2

CHAPTER FIFTEEN

Fifteenth Teaching

Can you live like no lives
have been lived?

How is this done?

Through holding onto the One true source of power. The only true source of power. By holding onto the One truth, encompassing all truths.

What is this power and truth?

This moment. This all-encompassing state of presence where no time can touch.

When alignment with the source of all can be felt, there is no longer a need for creation on the outer realm. You achieve inner, lessen outer.

All is well when this moment arises and this moment is felt with full being and this moment alone is where attention is focused.

Holding deep to all that is, there is no longer a heaviness of mind, controlling thought and action. Thought and action arise from a place of true power: from Truth itself.

Can you be alone and yet together with all? Can you hold onto the togetherness yet find the Oneness within it?

Seeking, swaying to and fro can leave only traces of that which contains within it all the power of the universe.

Be silent and still with the beauty and wonder of creation, and all is well.

Enjoy the outer play, go deep within, through inner awareness, through the love of all.

Spend time within True Self in the realm of no time. The paradox of outer and inner can be revealed as nothing more than a paradox of the game of life itself.

Can you be as a newborn baby can be? Can you look upon the outer with love, wonder and compassion? Can you feel this moment as all there is and all there ever will be?

Needing, wanting, seeking, holding onto past and future can serve no gain.

Use what you need when holding true.

This includes what is known to you through the faith that is already held onto.

Can you be with the calling to awaken?

Can you be with the calling to see the truth and to forever be at One with what is?

You need to come forward and take your place.

How long do you want to continue this turning from your true destiny?

Leave what is not, for all that what is.

For you cannot be away from the One for long, not ever, not when there is so much to give.

So give now what there is to be told. This world

can be forsaken for the depths it has gone. But now it must change to behold the depths it can go.

There is no need of the ages to say what is true. For the truth is within, it is inside of you.

Take hold of it now, for the now is what is and what is can be held within all that can be.

Love and be loved.

How can it be when the poor are for living as the rich are too poor?

Seek nothing; seek no loving of image and gain and prosperity, for these will only hold back what can be.

Use that which can be used for the greater good. Use not that which can be used for the greater need. The need of all wants and wants of all needs can be of no service to that which is ready.

Ready for the one, the one that is all, the one that can wait for the all to befall. For to befall is to gain and to gain is to love, and what is the universe without love from above?

Can the love that is One reach the love that has none? For the love that has none does not, will not, nor never will, behold the One. And the love that has not, cannot, nor shall not ever be within what is One.

Hold true to that which cannot be grasped tightly, for the yielding of form is what form is to water, and water cannot be held through the tight fists that grasp.

This water is the life, the life we all behold, and this life can be felt but not ever grasped tight.

For to grasp is to seek and to seek is to fail, and through failing there is no need for the seeing eyes to prevail.

For there is no failure within the eyes of the Lord, and the eyes of the Lord seek no happening, seek no truth.

But the truths that will be, can be seen, can be felt, for the Lord loves no others than those that can be.

And to be is what covers the life in between.

Between worlds and all others that can be felt and can be seen.

To take and to grasp is to one thing not other, for to see and to love is the true nature of water.

And water holds true along the power within you, and the power that holds you is the truth inside you.

Take no heed for that to come for that is not done, for to hold to the future can be no more or less truer.

Truth as to air is the beauty within, and this beauty within can be held onto with no needing or waiting or seeking its truth, for this truth that is sought is already inside you.

Amen.

CHAPTER SIXTEEN

Sixteenth Teaching

Hi again, my friend.

All that is, when no mind is felt through holding within, that which is the truth, can be utilized in ways for the greater to all good.

Who seeks then finds is who thinks then feels.

So many come to seek yet so many come undone to all that is, that of the One.

When Oneness and Beingness can hold together the outer and inner, complete perfection is present.

This presence of perfection is not close to that which the mind perceives as perfection. This perfection is Truth itself, is Love, Peace and Oneness. That doesn't mean it reflects perceived perfection on the outer realm, although this can and often is the case.

Perfection in true sense is that which can bring together the beauty of inner with the challenges of outer. These two can intertwine in loving embrace, and all that this touches can be one within God's grace.

To see and to feel, to touch and to hold, this all-encompassing Loveness and Oneness is mastery of Self, is mastery of All. It is the mastery where no other mastery is required.

Going deep and holding true to peace within can only be done when mind is overcome. For mind can not perceive that what it needs, and what it needs is not lost but hidden deep within one's Self.

To love and live through this love is purpose fulfilled.

On outer stay true and inner go through. Go through to the depths of all wonder creation.

Creation is there so one can foresee and hold dear to the truth that we are all One without fear.

For fear no longer serves what is needed on Earth, it is fear of the mind that needs to unwind and unwinding at will is not for the mind to instil. The being beneath is that which can set free all its creatures, and all its creatures when living with this will have naught but peace, true love, and true bliss.

Come forth through the light, which is still within earthly delight, and one's true Self is given the Oneness realm of no thing.

No thing is bliss and its bliss is eternal. Eternal goodness, what more can be yearned?

When staying present through challenge there is no need for one to suffer. A challenge presents when a challenge is sought not on level of mind but deep in from below.

Without challenge, where would there be a need to go deep? To go deep is what is, what is that which all is to become.

Can you be one with life, within all, within light. There is no way other than for this to discover.

To love and to live through Oneness within, one can stay true to Oneself. The Oneself that is all.

Staying true to Oneself allows that which is needed to come forth and be lived, through no thought longer seeded.

Stay light, stay true, stay deep inside you, and this light can come through you to dwell all around this divine, heavenly earthly realm.

CHAPTER SEVENTEEN

Seventeenth Teaching

> It is time to start going deeper, to start
> living as much within as without.

Can you feel the Oneness inside? Can you go deeper and deeper still into the realm of the Infinite and the Eternal?

You can and you do now go deeper. Stay in touch with that which is pure and true in depth.

Start living in the true flow of all. The sensory delights are not to be found without going very deep. Deeper than experiences up to now have led.

Stay close within this flow knowing all is well, and all is for the better good of all.

Trust more deeply, forever more deeply.

Feel the flow, and be One with it.

This Oneness flow will lead you into the great depths of wonder, that are there not only to be discovered and embraced but to be felt on the Oneness plane of all.

When one can feel full beauty, one can offer this beauty to others, to all that connect with it.

Aspiration and inspiration will be of no problem when trusting the deep flow of all things and of no things.

Low level unease, boredom, and discontent can only arise when you are not within the full flow of life.

To go deep within this flow one must trust very deeply, be very open to it and acknowledge it with gratitude.

Is more needed to be written?

This is an ongoing process of awakening to what is. The more that is written can be of no harm and of infinite assistance. But one must read and trust in these teachings, otherwise one cannot live them.

Keep writing, keep living that which is written.

The sunshine of love.

The flowering of beauty.

The one meets the other and all is at ease.

All is one fullness, of joy, of love, of light and true happiness.

Hold the sunshine of true love within, and all will be well without.

CHAPTER EIGHTEEN

Eighteenth Teaching

What shall I do?

You need to start.

You need to watch the patterns of your mind, the way they can construct pain, pain that is not necessary. Trust that what you are doing right now is perfect. Do not let mind come in at the subconscious level and start creating pain. Pain for what? Worry about what?

Trust in life.

One with all.

What do I do about the situation?

Just follow your heart, follow your true mind,

you can make no mistakes—all is as it should be and will be.

It is a time to grow when this type of pain comes up. Why is it there? What can be felt? Can you go deeply into it and watch it dissipate? Are you going to let it control your thinking, control your feelings?

Be one with it, grow with it, it is there within perfection—learn from it.

CHAPTER NINETEEN

Nineteenth Teaching

*Hi, what shall I do in
regards to moving forward?
Is it fear stopping me?*

Firstly, there is no need to resist within. Within knows, and within is perfection. Every thought is assisting which the mind cannot comprehend. Use your skills openly and without fear, there is no need for fear.

Trust that you will be guided perfectly in every way, in every feeling and every thought. Fear can be overcome when it is felt.

To feel incomplete can be used as a sign that it's time to move. Watch your thoughts and watch your feelings.

Use your fear as a teacher—do this through acknowledging the feeling as soon as it arises, then push through and continue. Will is found through this way.

You can be of great service in any area. Start anywhere that feels right, see where it leads. The journey cannot be imagined by mind and if it is, borders and obstacles are unnecessarily created—although all this is one with perfection in the wider sense.

Just trust you will be guided along every step. Trust that there is nothing to fear, no failure to be of concern. There is no failure, only the steps taken in the journey that is life.

Grow and trust, trust and grow.

Watch your thoughts more closely—grow in awareness, do not be lazy in this process.

Will will come when will is needed. Do not allow mind to create the resistance between what mind thinks and what the journey is at this moment.

Work will be found when work is sought. If you do not seek it, it cannot be found.

Like in the inner life seeking must and will turn to finding, but if you do not take the necessary steps, each one taken in the now, then this work you know you are capable of cannot eventuate. You must trust in each step—this fear of failure is a phantom thought stream that is no longer serving you.

Be aware of the thoughts, feel deeply the feelings. Do no resist, do not hide away, do not run from these thoughts and feelings. Embrace them lightly, know them not to be of truth. Trust in the path. Trust in creation of this specific path. Act through feeling in this moment—do not allow mind to continually procrastinate—for to procrastinate is to allow fear its sticking ways. This fear is of no help, its only value being as a signpost.

This fear would not be if on a deeper level you know you are ready to move forward in this sense. This knowing results in mind creating fear and bringing up the fears of failure from the past. These two opposing forces of knowing and fear create pain, much pain. Are you not ready to move on from this pain? Are you wanting to create more of this pain?

You have unlimited potential—why not use this? Why not be an asset to this world of creation? To not go out into the world with love and Oneness is to not physically spread this love and Oneness.

This uncertainty and fear that you can now acknowledge, become One with it, consciously try creating more of it and let it burn up into the light. You can have satisfaction on the outer level by trusting deeply that all is well, that no mistakes can be made, that failure is a phantom ghost of mind creation.

Will, will be there when trusting in this.

Fear of the unknown is perfectly natural for all humans yet there is no need for it. Why not embrace the unknown in the full trust embrace of the Divine?

Trust deeply and all will be well, all must be well, all is well. Much love and happiness, no more do you need to resist and hide—be open and be free.

CHAPTER TWENTY

Twentieth Teaching

Only within the Oneness realm
can there be true love,
compassion and goodwill.

Use your inner motivations to enjoy this realm, to give this to others.

Trust where there is this love, this Oneness, this compassion. Trust that you are this.

Discoveries of beauty and of true bliss sit eternally within this Oneness plane; you are at home in this realm.

There is no higher gift than the gift of wonder at God's creation in this heavenly realm of wonder and bliss.

You can see this deep within, and you can go to this place of wonder when times are at their point of learning and discovery.

Never mind the energies that the mind can perceive as bad or negative, never mind in those feelings of heaviness, of guilt or fear. They are yours to grow from, they are yours to explore. They carry within as much goodness as any and all experiences to be had in the Earth-bound dimension of time.

Use your gifts wisely, trusting the path deep within. Spread the love and the compassion liberally and acknowledge the goodness within others, within all life forms, within all of creation.

You will have what is needed when it is needed, remember this.

So long is there a need for suffering, for pain, for the ills of this world, this need you are no longer bound to. Appreciate it when it comes, but you can now move through it with ease and lightness of the Oneness-heart.

The love you feel is God's love and God's love is within all.

Trust all that is experienced is the exact experience to be welcomed within and without in this present moment.

Love all.

Where one can feel with all the love of God, one can be at true peace within and without.

To do this, one does not need to do anything but to acknowledge the beauty and perfection within each moment.

You are growing in wisdom and in maturity. You are growing in light and in love. You are growing in harmony, in perfect synchronicity with the all that is. There is no need for worries although worries are, of course, a part of this growth.

You can rest easy in the knowledge that all is okay, that all is happening as it is, and that you are on the right path of love and Oneness.

To know this is to be within the love of God itself. To be this is to be One with God himself and to do his work through the One love of all.

No longer does fear need to rule.

You have suffered, now prosper. Prosper in the heart, prosper in the joy of giving selflessly to those who are within your reach of beingness.

Compassion arises when love of all is within your Oneness-heart.

Show what is shown through this Oneness-love, and all will be well within and without.

CHAPTER TWENTY-ONE

Twenty-First Teaching

How do I make big life decisions?

Only you can make these decisions through love and knowing that all is okay, there is no wrong decision. Your lack of motivation is a sign of being overtaken, by the fear to move forward in your outer life. This can be worked through by trusting more deeply. This may not seem easy, but remember all this is unimportant on the larger scale of your existence. Whatever you do, it does not matter; it is not of absolute importance. Whatever road that is chosen to be travelled will be the right one.

Why am I so scared?

You are too stuck in your mind, too stuck in future, even too stuck to trust in this.

When you can be at one with your true Self, you are in alignment with the power of all.

CHAPTER TWENTY-TWO

Twenty-Second Teaching

You can use the tools you have
learnt to start living in a way which
intensifies your soul growth.

How do I do this?

You do this through listening deep within whenever you can. Follow the depths of your true being. Only when you do this will you be fulfilled and in a closer relationship with the Divine. This relationship is never closed, however it can be intensified through listening to the depths of your being.

When all is at one within, the need for worry, for depression, for the anxieties of the outer world no longer overcome your true nature.

Through being close with being, one can be closer to following true paths of purpose on the outer realm.

Everything that is being experienced is part of this, but active deepening of this path can be achieved through going deep, and trusting all that is within the true depths of you at this moment.

To be One with all is to be in a place of ease and lightness, trust and in full faith of all that is.

CHAPTER TWENTY-THREE

Twenty-Third Teaching

Hi again, my friend.

When all can be seen through that which is, at the level of true being, one can be entwined in ease, lightness and all of God's graces.

One should always continue forth holding trust deep within. Trust in the knowing that all is well within and without.

The need for despair can only end in the need for peace.

What you can do is at One with what can be done within all. There is only a need for what can be followed within the depths of being.

This inner pilot of your soul will lead where and when it has trust of depth and active attention within. While one may travel far, one may not see the needs of all those who one can be of assistance to.

When there is a beacon afar and the light is within, all can be at one with true purpose.

The love that can be reached, the love that can be given and expressed is the love that all have within. It is now the depths of this love that are to be explored and embraced.

To have and to hold onto this love is to be within the true presence of the Divine. Persistence and patterns will be of utmost importance and will assist with true soul growth and journeys forward.

To know the depths of true Self is to be found through trust. This trust can be found through knowing the depths of your true Self. To know this is to know that. Where there is only one there cannot be the other, but to know one is to know the other. To reach this, there is no reaching but the knowing within.

PART 3

CHAPTER TWENTY-FOUR

Twenty-Fourth Teaching

When one can see the wonders of this moment, when one can be at One with all that is, then one can not only follow the true path of that which is true love, true knowing, true life itself, but one can also be within the love of God and to feel this within all fullness.

Help to others is true help to self. For to help another is to help the lives of all that are living, have lived, and will live. To show true love, to show true trust in another, is to be within all creational love that is.

You are no longer needing the growth of pain, of suffering, of ignorant hearts. You can now move forward, move through and move upwards into the realm of true being and true knowing.

This is done through becoming forever closer to the source of all love and wonder, and this will always be of your true nature within and without.

All gifts are given when all time is of no time, and all trust is felt when life itself is lived through the Oneness realm of holy creation and wonder.

You have what is said to be that which is sought and loved by all beings, within all worlds, within all realms of truth.

Leave that which is no longer feeling of truth, that which is no longer seeding true love and true joy. Leave that which is of the mind and its dissoluteness.

No longer is being a fantasy of mind, as you begin to step into realms of consciousness that can only result in an intensifying of true love and true joy. All of this results in an acceleration of growth within, and growth within results in true growth without.

To love fully is to be the stream of all streams within the vast currents of all life's forces, and all life's forces emanate from the same large pool of existence. And this pool is within all pools of the manifested sea of beauty, love and wonder. And this beauty of love and wonder is within the flood of all floods and love of all loves, the God of all creation, the Source that is of all.

When moving deeper into realms of true mystery, embrace the trusting heart within and go forever deeper into love and beauty of the one true Self.

CHAPTER TWENTY-FIVE

Twenty-Fifth Teaching

When opening the heart of all hearts, sit within the Oneness plane of all that exists. All that exists is all there has been, is and will be in the one true dimension of no time. No time can only be experienced through going deep, to depths only attainable through conscious awareness, through conscious breathing, through consciousness living as One.

Silence is experienced through this depth, joy is felt deep and the knowing is known as the truth of all, and all is of the perfection of the One Divine presence of all.

To sit in this silence is to sit in the hands of God, and to sit in the hands of God one can be of no thing but of all things, heavenly in nature and yet of no thing within itself.

No thing can only be experienced when no thing is held within in the confines of all that is.

To stay true to the nature of the Divine is not only your true home of divinity, it is also the place of true sacredness where all can be felt within and without.

All that is experienced on levels yet unfathomable to the mind is experienced through the deepest levels of trust, through the deepest levels of love and bliss, and that which can only be experienced as the joy of God.

When one sits in this way, one loves all within and without. One loves the troubles of mind, one loves the play of creation, one loves the depths of being and the truth within all truths.

Go deep.

Trust.

Silence those thoughts through accepting them for what they are—their nature of impermanence and of their desire to define and separate. Notice their nature, their pull of mind energy this way and that. Notice their need for attention and, most of all, notice the strong pull and need for identification and reaction.

CHAPTER TWENTY-SIX

Twenty-Sixth Teaching

You will see the lights of all destinies held firm in the loving embrace of the One at times of true love and wholeness. This embrace of love and full truth is an embrace which transcends all the mind's fragile misperceptions of that which is true life in its wholeness and full beauty.

Soon, when no longer the mind can interfere, all joy, all wonder, all true passion of the One, the Holy will be felt at depths within, quite incomprehensible by the human mind and it's fragile pillars of belief and ignorance thoughts.

When laying down to sleep, go deep. Go fully into the realms of no mind, wonder and bliss.

Explore and welcome the infinite discoveries of truth and love, explore the depths beyond depths and the love of all loves. Soon this welcome of truth and love will encompass all areas of daily living but for now explore it most fully when welcoming the return sleep of source creation.

Standing tall, standing strong, standing within the knowledge of true power and innocence one will be that power, wisdom and love. For to stand in this way is to transform one's life from a dimension of mind to a realm where no time is sought where no love can be tarnished and where all Oneness is felt.

So soon can one be within this blissful realm for as soon as mind is transcended this dimension of true life is what is left. It is a dimension of truth and wholeness that gives out with the love and full embrace of all God's creatures.

To experience forever deeper one must first burn up the mind and its creations. To burn up is to be in full awareness, to give the mind and its tools full light of knowingness that one is not the mind. It is to feel fully the emotions within the body—the past thoughts and beliefs that no longer serve a necessary purpose.

To love fully is to be fully, and to be fully is to merge into the full embrace of God's creational vibration. When this is done, only what is true and of full love can be experienced, for this is the only experience of full trueness. Trust in this, and your life will be full of glory, wonder and joy. Fear is no longer given its illusory power, a power that once purpose is fulfilled can no longer be of service to the transcendence of time and its illusions.

Stand strong, stand within all, love like no love, other than the love of All, the love of Oneness within and without of all that has been, is, and will forever be.

To look deeply into self is to merge with truth. To merge with truth is to acknowledge that there is only One God, and that God is of all things and no things. Nothingness within everything and everything within no thing. Be One, for One is all there is and love is true energy radiating within and without all creations, of all spiritual dimensions within the One dimension of love.

So to keep living in mind is to keep living in ignorance, and this is the one thing that is no longer required. Be strong within the trust that all is well, all is of perfection, the journey is only now, and now is all there is. Stay strong transcendentally through the working of mind energy, and all will come to you and to all of God's creations, when all is felt within and without.

So for now, keep holding true to your loving truth of hearts deep within. The mind and its creations hold no true power compared to holding close and true through the love of the Divine.

CHAPTER TWENTY-SEVEN

Twenty-Seventh Teaching

When enjoying the pleasures of life, go deep within the body. Go as deeply as you can and feel the vibrational movement within. This movement, this true being below the external reality is your true nature, the true energy of the Divine.

When this can be felt and embraced, the pulls of the external world can only cause ripples on the surface of your deep sea. The ripples are noticed immediately, they are noticed through full awareness. If they are resulting in negative emotion, this negative emotion is embraced with full love and attention, and transmutation of low vibration to high vibration can unfold.

Trust that you are being led perfectly, all are being led perfectly through the experience on the inner and outer that is necessary for true spiritual growth to unfold.

This spiritual growth is the true growth of becoming One with all that is, with the divine nature of true reality itself. When you trust in life, life gives all necessary experiences with ease and can unfold these experiences toward you more easily resulting in a quickening of growth, all in perfect alignment with what you need to go through and experience at this moment.

So stay fully in the trust embrace of the flow of life itself. The more you trust in this, the more you let it guide your thoughts and actions, the closer you are to full transcendence, the closer you are to joy, to true bliss and a deep peace and harmony within and without of all.

Hold strength within this Oneness-heart, for all strength is within this strength and your experiences in the earthly realm can unfold with ease.

These experiences are not always designed for ease and complacency; these experiences are there for growth and deepening of aspiration toward true love of all. Therefore these experiences may at times be judged by the mind as difficult, challenging and even very painful. This is all perfect; the sooner one shows strength to move through these more challenging outer life experiences, the sooner one can enjoy the full knowing of Oneness and love within all. The sooner one can enjoy sitting, being and embracing the Divine.

So see life's troubles as a beautiful thing, know this when times seem tough. Never let these tough times take the true you beneath the mind fully over, as to bring full awareness to these times is to bring the power and beauty of God to assist in transmuting and transcending these challenging times of pain growth.

Through the trust that all is well, all is perfect for you and for all, deeply and in full love, these surface challenges can be embraced and moved through with ease. The more this is done, the stronger you become and a point soon comes where a problem, a crisis, a challenge is acknowledged fully, is embraced with a smile, and is transcended through the power of full awareness with ease. This is the art of true living and much joy and love can be brought to even the most challenging of times. Trust in this deeply.

Keep raising the awareness of mind, keep growing in spiritual power through transcending the mind and it's challenges whenever possible.

Remember, full awareness, full love, full acceptance is all that is ever needed for full joy, beauty, and true love to shine fully through.

CHAPTER TWENTY-EIGHT

Twenty-eighth Teaching

When following the depths of Self, one does not need to concentrate attention on those things which are not necessary at this moment. Planning happens but planning need not take energy from present moment awareness into the idea of future. To grow fully is to face challenges with a loving embrace. And to grow is to encounter things which can seem like obstacles but are there for growth to transmute fully.

Life is here and now, life is what you are, and life is what you will always be. Trust in this. Trust in the step you take right now. Trust that it will lead you perfectly.

Can you transcend openly, honestly and with the support of full life strength itself?

There is an opening into the formless that can only get larger as true strength is brought to all challenges faced. You can grow in alignment with life itself when full surrender to each moment is felt within and without.

Do you trust enough in every moment? Is there fear of the unknown and fear of failure? Is there fear of that which can only be called, the need for perfection? This fear is of the mind. It holds no truth, it holds no power except when power is given from you.

Resistance is felt when the mind creates fear of failure, of imperfection, of wrong action and mistakes being made. These fears are all illusory; none of these exist in reality. Trust in this.

CHAPTER TWENTY-NINE

Twenty-Ninth Teaching

Hi, my friend

Can I ask you anything?

Yes.

What shall I ask you?

Ask me whatever is of interest to you deep down, ask what will move you forward and move you forever more deeply into the realm of infinite depth.

Ask the questions that will transform lives.

The first question you could ask: What is the purpose of life?

The purpose of life is twofold. Firstly, the purpose of life is to experience full soul growth through travelling to the depths of love, light and bliss within. This Oneness within then corresponds to outer reality.

The second purpose of life is found through knowing the utmost depths of creational wonder. This creational wonder is known when all is in the One alignment of true life. This alignment is to be at a time when all is well, all is love, and all is the truth of all truths. This second purpose cannot be comprehended fully or explained through the mind. This second purpose is one that only the truth within your soul can relate to in fullness.

The second question you may want to ask is: If life is for growth and for knowledge, why is this earthly realm necessary for these things?

The earthly realm is necessary for three main reasons. Firstly, the sensations, the hardships, the pleasures, the fundamental laws are all governed in a way that is unique to this earthly realm. Therefore, this realm has specific purposes that can be attributed and used toward soul growth and specific knowings.

Secondly, time on this earth is necessary for the reunited love of those long known. The people you encounter in your outer life are souls you have encountered many times before. Earth becomes a meeting place for souls to rekindle that which has not been rekindled in some time. True love can be found with greater ease when among those you have loved and known for a long time, for many lives and in many worlds. You might say the souls you encounter in this realm have previously made an agreement with you to enter this realm at this time so a reunion in this realm becomes possible.

Thirdly, this earthy realm is necessary for true and rapid soul growth. The battles faced and hardships lived are all within the perfection of that which is necessary for your soul at this time. While the hardships are of utmost importance, the positive growth that comes out of these hardships while on Earth is of infinite value and creates a love like no other. While this world can be tough, this world is like all worlds—based upon pure love, joy and bliss. And through hardships, this love, joy and bliss can be forever further expanded within and experienced. So embrace the pains, troubles and hardships for the blessing of God is carried within every one.

The third and final question you may like to ask is: How long do we stay in this realm and what comes next?

The length of stay is dependent on your soul's growth and development, and dependant on the choices made before entering this earthly realm. It is also dependant on those souls around you who you love and have known for many eons. Your soul has some time in this realm yet, and the true flowering of love, joy and bliss is going to create some phenomenal experiences while you are in this realm.

What happens after leaving this earthly realm is twofold. Firstly you will go through a transitional period of adaptive growth where the soul can get used to the next realm of consciousness. This will be for as long as is necessary, although for you this will not be a long time. After this transitional period you go to a realm quite indescribable to the earthly mind.

This place is of the most pure love, light and of blessings all around. The transitional period is needed because of the intensity of this pure love, grace and Oneness with God. This realm is for those who have become soul ready, and for those who are now at One with the true glory, the true love, the true magnificence of the beauty of life itself.

The life that is the Supreme.

CONTACT

To reach the author, please email
hiddentruthswithin@mail.com.
Thank you.

ALYBLUE MEDIA TITLES

PARTIAL LIST

Who Took Holly Piirainen?
Weird Girl Adventures
She, He & Finding Me
Letters to Matt
Survivors
Faces of Resilience
Barely Breathing
Who Took Molly Bish?
Color My Soul Whole
Remembering My Child
My Grief Diary
Grammy Visits From Heaven
Grandpa Visits From Heaven
Daddy Visits From Heaven
Faith, Grief & Pass the Chocolate Pudding
Crimson Sunshine
Heaven Talks to Children
A Child is Missing: A True Story
A Child is Missing: Searching for Justice
Grief Reiki
Where have all the children gone?

GRIEF DIARIES

Surviving Loss by Overdose
Surviving Sudden Loss
Through the Eyes of a Widow
Surviving Loss by Cancer
Surviving Loss of a Spouse
Surviving Loss of a Child
Surviving Loss of a Sibling
Surviving Loss of a Parent
Surviving Loss of an Infant
Surviving Loss of a Loved One
Surviving Loss by Suicide
Surviving Loss of Health
How to Help the Newly Bereaved
Surviving Loss by Impaired Driving
Surviving Loss by Homicide
Surviving Loss of a Pregnancy
Hello from Heaven
Grieving for the Living
Project Cold Case
Poetry & Prose and More
Through the Eyes of Men
Will We Survive?
Victim Impact Statement
Surviving Loss of a Pet

INTERNATIONAL GRIEF INSTITUTE

Aftercare Solutions Manual
Certified iCare Specialist Manual
Compassion Fatigue
iCare Grief Support Group Facilitator Manual
iCare Grief Support Participant Workbook
iCare Church Support Facilitator Manual
iCare Church Support Participant Workbook
iCare Grief Ministry Guide
iCare Grief Workbook
iCare Chapter Manual

Humanity's legacy of stories and storytelling
is the most precious we have.

DORIS LESSING
*

PUBLISHED BY ALYBLUE MEDIA
Inside every human is a story worth sharing.
www.AlyBlueMedia.com

www.ingramcontent.com/pod-product-compliance
Lightning Source LLC
Chambersburg PA
CBHW031450040426
42444CB00007B/1040